BRIAN JOHNSTON

Songs of Zion

An Exploration of True Biblical Worship

Contents

1

Worshipping in Submission

Our aim in this study will be to spend time considering the true nature of biblical Christian worship by paying attention to the words and ideas used in the Bible for worship. Biblically, worship may be summed up in two words, and so let's look at the first of those words.

The first of the two main ideas we can associate with biblical worship (Hebrew: *shāchāh*; Greek: *proskuneō*) is the idea of 'submission.' In both parts of the Bible, a common word for worship means to 'bend over' or 'bow down.' In other words, it describes a gesture of respect or submission. We find Moses in Exodus 34:8 making haste to bow low and worship (*shāchāh*). And Jesus in Luke 4:8 quotes Deuteronomy 6:13: "*You shall worship (proskuneō) the Lord your God and serve Him only.*" Here also 'worship' has the sense of submission. Earlier in the same chapter from which Jesus was quoting, Moses had told the Israelites: "*You shall love the LORD your God with all your heart and with all your soul and with all your might*" (Deuteronomy 6:5). To truly love the Lord demands nothing less than our all.

It's not possible for us to love the Lord in this way and, at the same time, be chasing after the things of the world. Love of God and love of the world are incompatible, for the Apostle John says: *"If anyone loves the world, the love of the Father is not in him"* (1 John 2:15). Those verses from Deuteronomy chapter 6 not only warn us against having divided affection and loyalties – but also show us that wholehearted love for God precedes and underpins genuine worship of God; we read *"love the Lord your God"* before we read *"worship the Lord your God."* They get mentioned in that order. Worship is born out of loving submission. Love and worship belong together – and this must surely also apply in the mistaken case of loving the world. Let me unpack that.

Through our own greed, lust and pride, the world draws us away, and we end up compromising our love for the Lord. What's really going on when that happens? The world is competing with God for our attention and allegiance. Whom or which will we submit to? God or the world? It takes effort to obtain the desirable things this world offers, such as fame, success and financial rewards. The effort it takes to get these things distracts us from allegiance to God, and so dilutes our affection for God. The result is that what we desire and become devoted to, and the worldly goal we submit ourselves to reaching, actually defines whom it is that we worship. And the choice is between God and whoever is behind the interests, ambitions and values of this world.

Let's try to make this even clearer. In Luke chapter 4, we find the Devil trying to get Jesus to worship him. You'll remember the scene: the three temptations which the Devil put to our Lord Jesus at the close of the 40 days of special testing at the beginning of our Lord's public life. In reply, Jesus used this word for worship – the one with the idea of submission – when he answered the Devil's temptation by saying: *"You shall worship (Gk. proskuneō) the Lord your God, and serve Him only"* (Luke 4:8, from Deuteronomy 6:13). This was said immediately after the Devil had – quite literally – promised Jesus the world in exchange for Jesus being prepared to worship him and submit his allegiance to Satan.

Of course, we have to recognize this was a very specific temptation, made in special circumstances. But having said that, doesn't it seem to further imply that it's within Satan's power to grant worldly honours (such as gain and glory) for which submission to his authority is his asking price? If so, doesn't it indicate that 'worship' of the Devil, in this sense of submission, takes place whenever a person finds their satisfaction in worldly attractions, attitudes and ambitions? After all, the whole world lies in the power of the evil one (1 John 5:19). In this case, the lifestyle choice which the Bible presents us with is stark in its extremes.

Perhaps a compromise position is more common: one in which we find ourselves being partly yielded in practice to the Devil's authority and partly yielded to the Lord's authority. This will reflect our love being, in part, for the things of the world. We still crave – in some degree – the applause and accolades of the world that doesn't know the Lord. The worship which the Devil is shown to seek after is achieved if we should align ourselves with that world's values and beliefs. The same choice that was presented to the Lord is therefore the same as is set before us by Paul in a more general way in Romans 12, by James in James 4 and by John in 1 John 2. These texts warn us against conforming our attitudes to the world, and against being attracted to having friendship with the world and against entertaining worldly ambitions. But isn't this the same basic issue? How far in the direction of giving the Devil what he's looking for does conforming to the world, having unqualified friendship with worldly people and entertaining love for the world's attractions take us? And what the Devil is looking for is our worship, our submission, to his influence.

All of what we're saying will, one day, and much less subtly, be seen in the future crisis prophesied in the book of Revelation. A time is coming when cooperation in the world's religion, economics and politics will only be secured when a person is prepared to worship openly the so-called beast or Antichrist (who will be Satan's man or proxy). Unfortunately, many believers now, lacking an understanding of the underlying biblical meaning of worship, get caught up with trying to 'live the dream' down here by sacrificing time and effort to get ahead – to gain worldly things – without realizing that in some sense and in some degree they've stepped into an alternative form of worship, irrespective of how orthodox their views may be and regardless of how faithful their church attendance is. It's about where our mindset or focus is – whether on things above or confined to what's under the heaven.

Turning now from Luke chapter 4 to John chapter 4, we find here that it's now no longer the Devil but it's the Father (that is, God the Father) who's seeking worshippers. Those who yield their wills to his will by worshipping his way, receive the privilege of experiencing an amazing access into heaven as they now serve the Lord from within a spiritual house on earth. However, let's not leap ahead too far just yet, but begin by noting that the word for worship here in John 4 is again the worship word which means submission which we previously saw used in Luke 4.

Well, it's time to look at that New Testament word more closely. This original Bible word is made up of the preposition 'towards' and the verb 'to kiss.' That verb – to kiss – in turn comes from the word for a 'dog' by means of the idea of it 'licking a hand.' It could then mean that the basic meaning of our featured worship word came from the idea of bowing down before someone and kissing his feet, or the hem of his garment, or even the ground in front of him. In the Greek version of the Old Testament, it's used, about 75% of the time to express worship either of God or indeed of the pagan gods. (At other times its use is to express the general idea of bowing to show respect to a person in any position of authority.)

I'll give you some examples of the word being used to express the idea of worship to the God of Israel: e.g. the servant of Abraham bowed down in worship of the Lord after he found a wife for Isaac, his master's son (Genesis 24:26). The Israelites in Egypt bowed in worship to God when they heard God was going to deliver them (Exodus 4:31). And it was used again during the dedication of Solomon's Temple – when the people saw the temple filled with the glory of the Lord and fell face down on the ground worshipping the Lord (2 Chronicles 7:3). All of which conveys to us the idea that when used to describe worship it is a word which represents both the outward physical expression and the internal attitude of reverent submission on the part of the worshipper.

It's important to understand that the Old Testament establishes the idea of worship as embracing a submission that's expressed both physically and is also spiritual, being from the heart as when we read: "the people bowed low and worshiped" (Exodus 12:27). This same meaning of complete reverent submission is carried over into the New Testament where the word (*proskuneō*) is found mostly in the books of Matthew, John and Revelation.

To conclude our study on worship as submission, let's look at several examples of worship in the New Testament when it was being expressed toward the Lord in his public ministry on earth. In Matthew 2:1-2, it's recorded that Magi came from the East to Jerusalem and said, *"Where is He who has been born King of the Jews? For we saw His star in the east, and have come to worship Him."* This same term 'worship' or 'submission' is again used in Matthew 2:11: *"Having come into the house, the Magi found the child with Mary His mother, and having fallen down they worshipped Him."* That is, they expressed their reverence and submission to the one born King of the Jews. Matthew 8:1-2 tells of a leper who came to Jesus and was worshipping him, saying, *"If You are willing, You can make me clean."* The tense indicates that the leper started and kept on worshipping the Lord, expressing his reverence and submission by declaring that if the Lord should will, the Lord was able to cleanse him. His submission to the will of the Lord was expressed physically in his posture as well as being from his heart as indicated by the words of his mouth. These examples, directed towards the person of our Lord, set the tone for the use of this worship word in the rest of the New Testament.

Let's conclude this chapter with a wonderfully practical quote from William Temple that talks about worship as submission, our theme in this study: "Worship is the submission of all our nature to God. It is the quickening of conscience by His holiness; the nourishment of mind with His truth; the purifying of imagination by His beauty; the opening of the heart to His love; the surrender of will to His purpose – and all of this gathered up in adoration, the most selfless emotion of which our nature is capable and therefore the chief remedy for that self-centeredness which is our original sin and the source of all actual sin."

That really sums up the challenge to our hearts and minds of what true worship – viewed as true submission – actually looks like in practice!

2

Worshipping in Service

We've said that, biblically, worship may be summed up in two ideas that each draw support from the common words for worship in both parts of the Bible. In our previous study, we explored the idea of 'submission.' Now we'll take a look at the second idea of 'service' (Hebrew: *'abad*; Greek: *latreuō*).

In Exodus 20:5 (and in Deuteronomy 5:9), when the second of the famous Ten Commandments talks about neither worshipping nor 'serving' any graven image, it's this worship word that's used to express the Lord's command to serve only him (both ideas of submitting and serving found together here). On the brink of the Israelites finally setting foot in the Promised Land, they were told not to 'serve' other gods (Deuteronomy 4:16,19; 7:4,16). After the Lord had brought them in and defeated all of their enemies, Joshua says, *"Now, therefore, fear the LORD and serve Him in sincerity and truth; and put away the gods which your fathers served beyond the River and in Egypt; and serve the LORD"* (Joshua 24:14). Originally, this worship word which is often translated as 'serve' was in fact a secular term meaning to work for hire or wages; but in the Greek version of the Old Testament it's used to express either the worship of pagan gods or Israel's service of the true and living God.

Right away then, we're faced up with the basic fact that who or what we serve is the actual object of our worship. That is, what we devote our energies to is what or who we worship. As we begin to dig even deeper into the meaning of worship as service we need to take a look at the noun form of the word found in Romans 12:1-2 where Paul writes: "*Therefore I urge you, brethren, by the mercies of God, to present your bodies a living and holy sacrifice, acceptable to God, which is your spiritual service of worship. And do not be conformed to this world, but be transformed by the renewing of your mind, so that you may prove what the will of God is, that which is good and acceptable and perfect.*" Notice the expression Paul used there: "*your spiritual service of worship.*" I think that's worth exploring a little. I'd go so far as to say that there could be modern methods and styles of worship which would appear to be ruled out by this. For, when he writes: "*present your bodies a living sacrifice, holy, well-pleasing to God*" and then adds that's literally "your rational service" – Paul is telling us that worship definitely involves thinking through our response to God. In fact, worship is in harmony with the very highest form of reasoning, and is far from an unthinking emotional response or a mere ecstatic mood feeling, as some may think of it as being.

This brings us to another example of this worship word meaning 'service.' It's an example where we find it being used in a corporate sense to describe worship by God's Old Testament people, although the reference to it is in fact found in the New Testament. It's Romans 9, where Paul refers to: "*... my* *kinsmen ... to whom belongs ... the temple service"* (Romans 9:3-4). The reference is to Israel, but the very same word group translated here as 'service' (Gk. *latreia*) is also used of God's New Testament people also worshipping corporately in Philippians 3:3 where Paul says, *"we are the true circumcision, who worship in the Spirit of God and glory in Christ Jesus and put no confidence in the flesh."*

The worship of the people of God as expressed in this distinctive word – throughout all the Bible – is only ever directed to the God and Father of the Lord Jesus in the sense of *"you shall ... serve Him only"* (Luke 4:8). Now this in no way detracts, of course, from the fact that the Lord Jesus is himself truly God or from the fact that it was right for individuals who met him on earth to worship him, as we saw in our opening chapter. But it shows how it's no mere protocol or habit that those in biblical churches of God may very well address themselves to the One who is *"the God and Father of our Lord Jesus"* when coming together to worship God by keeping the Lord's command to break bread each Sunday morning.

Linking back to our reading in Romans 9:4 of the 'temple service' of God in a corporate sense by Israel, we find it goes right to the heart of a very important revelation regarding worship. That revelation is this: that there's worship that's to be corporately engaged in by the people of God – which in New Testament times answers to what was performed in Old Testament times by Israel. This is corporate worship that's distinct from the personal worship we can offer at any time, and it may in fact only accurately be offered to 'the Father'; that is, neither to the Lord Jesus nor to 'our Father' – but specifically to the God and

Father of our Lord Jesus.

According to Hebrews 2:12, our Lord Jesus is himself a worshipper who leads the congregation when it's singing praises! Basically, that's why New Testament churches of God were, and are, in existence! It's because God the Father wants this corporate worship from his people now, just as he received such worship from Israel in the past. We see this from John 4:23 when Jesus told the Samaritan woman at the well that the Father, his father, was seeking worshippers. In this worship today, the Lord Jesus is in the answering role to Aaron, Israel's high priest. The letter to the Hebrews teaches us that the worship offered by God's people ascends to God the Father through the Lord Jesus in his role as great priest over the house of God (Hebrews 10:21). This clear teaching further clarifies why the Lord Jesus is not the one to whom we specifically address ourselves in worship.

Nor do we call on God as our personal heavenly Father in this connection, but rather address him as the God and Father of our Lord who is our officiating high priest. This is his highest title. We are approaching not as God's scattered children but as his gathered people. That service of God in this sense which Israel previously offered – their collective worship as God's people – was expressed in the annual 'Feasts of Yahweh' (or perhaps better – though less accurately – known as the 'Feasts of Jehovah'). These 'feasts' were identified with *the Place of the Name*" (see Deuteronomy 12:5; 16:16) – which was then the unique place of God's own choosing and operated as the national centre for the people's worship of their God. This centre, of course, came to be identified with Jerusalem or Zion. Leviticus 23 gives the Lord's instruction to Moses in directing the nation's worship ...

> *"The LORD spoke again to Moses, saying, "Speak to the sons of Israel and say to them, 'The LORD'S appointed times which you shall proclaim as holy convocations – My appointed times are these: 'For six days work may be done, but on the seventh day there is a sabbath of complete rest, a holy convocation. You shall not do any work; it is a sabbath to the LORD in all your dwellings. These are the appointed times of the LORD, holy convocations which you shall proclaim at the times appointed for them.'"* (Leviticus 23:1-4).

This shows that these were occasions when the people of God came together - arranged meetings in which they came before him by his appointment. That's the meaning of this word 'feast.' A most remarkable feature of these feasts, running like a thread right down through them, was the command to remember. Without doubt, they find their counterpart during New Testament times in the weekly Breaking of the Bread (Acts 2:42) which is also an act of remembrance. No longer three times per year (Exodus 23:14) but once a week, we have such an appointment to keep and we, too, have not to come empty before him in worship, but to come with a sacrifice of praise to offer to God. This is the connection with what had gone before which we read about in Exodus 23:14-15...

> *"Three times a year you shall celebrate a feast to Me. You shall observe the Feast of Unleavened Bread; for seven days you are to eat unleavened bread, as I commanded you, at the appointed time in the month Abib, for in it*

you came out of Egypt. And none shall appear before Me empty-handed."

Obviously, we each have a duty, particularly those who vocally lead the worship, to appear before God full and fresh each week with a prepared, thoughtful scriptural meditation which expresses what we've been recently enjoying and full of the person of God's Son, Jesus. So, in the Old Testament, the people of God came together at the annual set feasts for collective worship. In the New Testament era, their counterpart in biblical churches of God is spoken of as their *"coming together"* at their weekly remembrance at the breaking of the bread (e.g. 1 Corinthians 11:17-18,20) for corporate worship.

A study of worship across the whole Bible is recommended as a sure way of confirming that God still intends there to be such a thing as a worshipping New Testament people of God as was found throughout the biblical churches of God two thousand years ago. That was then the exact counterpart of Israel and what they did in Old Testament times. In corporate, weekly worship, churches of God give the kind of worship that's expressed in this distinctive word for 'service' (Gk. *latreia*), which is exclusively for God the Father, and may be thought of as the highest expression of worship. This is not a matter of mere biblical interpretation, but is basic biblical exposition. Sadly, in all that is written today on worship practically nothing is to be found on this point of supreme importance.

3

The Old Testament Place of Worship

He probably liked his music loud – that's if the heavy metal emblem on his T-shirt was anything to go by. They made a strange looking pairing – this couple who were in earnest conversation: the young man with his wild, long hair, dressed in T-shirt and biker leathers, and the old missionary who was at this point acting as his spiritual counsellor at the close of an evangelical meeting in a big tent in the field beside the village. The old preacher had the right idea. He'd sensed the young man's interest in music. Optimistically, he asked him if he knew 'the songs of Zion.' The young man's eyes brightened as music certainly was his scene. He asked eagerly – and, I believe, innocently - "Can't say I've heard of them. Are they a new rock group?"

I guess that young man would be in good company. If the question was asked on a TV quiz show, 'What are the songs of Zion?' then how many would know the correct answer? Unless they could remember a hit song that was popular in my youth. It went by the title of 'By the Rivers of Babylon.' The lyrics were

– in part at least – a straight 'lift' from the Bible. It contained words from Psalm 137 set to modern reggae music. And the words were these:

> *By the rivers of Babylon, there we sat down and wept, when we remembered Zion. Upon the willows in the midst of it we hung our harps. For there our captors demanded of us songs, and our tormentors mirth, saying, "Sing us one of the songs of Zion!" How shall we sing the LORD's song in a foreign land?* (Psalm 137:1-4).

Picture the scene with me. The Jews had been defeated by the then world superpower of Babylon – we're talking nearly 600 years before Christ – and they'd been transported away from Jerusalem – away from the place where they'd known the worship of God at the magnificent temple built there by the famous and wise King Solomon. Their captors demanded from them the songs of Zion: songs with which God had been honoured in and around the temple-service at Jerusalem. But the captives had hung up their harps and they weren't going to oblige. It was as though they said: "How can we? It's the Lord's song; it's a sacred thing; it's really designed for the temple-service at Jerusalem, we daren't sing any of them in this foreign place. They don't belong here at all." And they certainly weren't going to use them to entertain their captors, even if they sang them quietly to themselves sometimes.

But, basically, the songs of Zion were songs that the Jews had sung in honour of God at Jerusalem. And the name Zion pretty well refers to Jerusalem – but we should check that out in a bit more detail. When Israel entered Canaan they took Jerusalem, but not the well-defended fortress of Jebus. It remained in the hands of the Jebusites, even though Benjamin occupied the surrounding area. This fortress is first called *"the stronghold of Zion"* in 2 Samuel (5:7) when we're told about its capture by David. Zion occupied the south-eastern hill of Jerusalem and it became known as *"the city of David."* The Bible seems then to indicate that, to start with at least, Zion wasn't completely identified with Jerusalem. But after the building of the Temple and the fetching of the Ark of the Covenant there, the name Zion came to refer to this place where God dwelt among his people.

Often Zion and Jerusalem are simply used in place of each other - and one of the psalms which mentions Zion tells us a bit more about the final stage of David bringing the Ark of the Covenant there. It's Psalm 132:

> *"Remember, LORD, in David's behalf, All his affliction; How he swore to the LORD And vowed to the Mighty One of Jacob, "I certainly will not enter my house, Nor lie on my bed; I will not give sleep to my eyes Or slumber to my eyelids, Until I find a place for the LORD, A dwelling place for the Mighty One of Jacob." Behold, we heard about it in Ephrathah, We found it in the field of Jaar. Let's go into His dwelling place; Let's worship at His footstool. Arise, LORD, to Your resting place, You and the ark of Your strength. For the LORD has chosen Zion; He has desired it as His dwelling place. This is My resting place forever; Here I will dwell, for I have desired it"* (Psalm 132:1-14).

Like God's choice of Abraham, God's choice of Zion is striking. For the hill of Zion is pretty insignificant compared to other hills, but whatever God selects becomes incomparably precious simply as a result of his having chosen it. That's something that we as Christians can enjoy (see Ephesians 1:4). Having chosen Israel as his people, and then having chosen David as someone through whom his purposes would be fulfilled, God next chose Zion. And the psalm we've read is just full of the joy that filled the people when the Ark of God was first taken there. This was the last stage of a journey which had begun at Sinai hundreds of years before – a journey that had seen the Ark travel through the desert and on in turn to Bethel, Shiloh, and Kiriath-jearim.

Psalm 132 describes the last lap in this long, interrupted journey as the Ark is taken in procession by David from Kiriath-jearim to the newly captured fortress. This was Mount Zion, chosen by God, and now the city of David. The sheer exhilaration felt by David, and the people, as the Ark of God entered Zion breathes through this psalm. First, David's deep heart-longing to secure a place for the Lord is described:

> *Remember, LORD, in David's behalf, all his affliction; how he swore to the LORD And vowed to the Mighty One of Jacob, "I certainly will not enter my house, nor lie on my bed; I will not give sleep to my eyes or slumber to my eyelids, until I find a place for the LORD, a dwelling place for the Mighty One of Jacob"* (Psalm 132:1–5).

David just couldn't sleep until he'd given God his rightful place. Then next comes an account of his search for the forgotten Ark – the Ark that had been ignored in King Saul's time. We learn of its discovery "in the field of the wood" which, from elsewhere in our Bibles, we can identify as Kiriath-jearim, the "city of woodlands."

> *"Behold, we heard about it in Ephrathah, We found it in the field of Jaar. Let's go into His dwelling place; Let's worship at His footstool. Arise, LORD, to Your resting place, You and the ark of Your strength"* (Psalm 132:6-8).

That last verse picks up and echoes Moses' words when the people and the Ark first set out from Sinai: *"Rise up, O LORD! And let Your enemies be scattered."* I believe that repetition is meant to show us that this last, six-mile journey was just the continuation of what was begun so long before. And the last few miles were as important to God as the first, for they were to end in the place which he'd chosen, the place that would be central to his purposes for long into the future.

David's love for God finds this 'response' from God (verses 13 and 14): *"For the LORD has chosen Zion; He has desired it as His dwelling place. This is My resting place forever; Here I will dwell, for I have desired it."* It's a 'response' on God's part that reaches far beyond the immediate occupation of a hilltop in Judah. *"Here will I dwell; for I have desired it"* stretches far beyond to include the glory of God's purposes involving the Messiah and his presence on earth during the Millennium when Zion will once again be central – and far more glorious than ever before. But there's even more than that to this idea of Zion as God's dwelling-place – there's so much more invested in this name of Zion – but we'll have to leave that discovery until a later study as we continue walking the highways to Zion, travelling along the pilgrim-ways leading us there.

4

A Worship Link Between Heaven & Earth

In the second-half of the nineteenth century, a Zionist society was founded in order to promote the idea of Jews resettling in the land of Palestine. At that time most Jewish people lived in Eastern Europe. While there, they set about reviving the old Hebrew language. A man called Eliezer Ben Yehuda was instrumental in this. He introduced it into his own home even though his wife objected that she couldn't even say 'I love you' in that language. She would just have to learn! It was largely due to this man's efforts that a generation of Jews was born which spoke Hebrew again as its old mother tongue.

Then in 1897, Theodor Herzl organized the first Zionist Congress. It was held in Switzerland. And he claimed at that time to have effectively established the Jewish state – something which, he predicted, would be recognized by all within fifty years. His optimism would prove to be well-founded when Israel was granted independence in 1948. And the rest, as they say, is history. Around the same time as this Zionist movement was getting underway, a group of Christians towards the close of the nineteenth century also had 'the highways to Zion' on their hearts – but in a spiritual sense. Both movements were movements of rediscovery. The one was about re-establishing *geographical* Zion; the other was concerned with rediscovering the truth about *spiritual* Zion – and it was bound up, of course, with the use of the word 'Zion' in our Bibles – as we, for example, find it used in Psalm 48:

> *"Great is the LORD, and greatly to be praised in the city of our God, in His holy mountain. Beautiful in elevation, the joy of the whole earth, is Mount Zion on the sides of the north, the city of the great King. God is in her palaces; he is known as her refuge"* (Psalm 48:1-3 NKJV).

Glorious things are spoken of Zion, the city of God (Psalm 87:3) – it's set on his holy mountain, and it's beautiful in elevation, the joy of the whole earth: that's mount Zion on the sides of the north. Curious expression that: "the sides of the north." Let me point you to another place in the Bible where that same expression is found. It's in the prophet Isaiah, chapter 14:

> *"... take up this proverb against the king of Babylon, and say: "How the oppressor has ceased, the golden city ceased! "How you are fallen from heaven, O Lucifer, son of the morning! How you are cut down to the ground, you who weakened the nations! For you have said in your heart: 'I will ascend into heaven, I will exalt my throne above the stars of God; I will also sit on the mount of the congregation on the farthest sides of the north; I will ascend above the heights of the clouds, I will be like the*

Most High" (Is.14:4,12-14 NKJV).

I hope you'll agree with me that the prophet's message contains references that can seemingly also apply to a being in heaven who is being addressed under the figure of the king of Babylon. On earth, there was a proud, arrogant king whom God was going to judge, and God uses him as a vehicle for revealing to us his judgement against the pride of some supernatural power. The pride of such a one in setting himself up as God's Adversary had been to say to himself: *"I will ascend into heaven, I will exalt my throne above the stars of God; I will also sit on the mount of the congregation on the farthest sides of the north."*

There's that linking expression – *"the sides of the north."* We recall how Psalm 48 had used it to describe geographical Zion. In other words, the psalmist was describing Jerusalem on earth, the Jerusalem city of his day. But as we're on the point of discovering, there's more to this name Zion than meets the eye at first glance. We say that because by comparing the wording of Psalm 48 and Isaiah 14 we can see that there's something in heaven – something in the very presence of God – of which Zion on earth must be a kind of reflection. You find this is confirmed from many different Bible verses other than this one in Isaiah 14.

But Isaiah 14 does picture for us God's own throne in heaven. The scene is that of God's holy hill above as being his seat of government and the true centre of worship – and it's spoken of as situated on the sides of the north – which is but one feature that links this heavenly Zion to its earthly counterpart. It's as though God's purpose has been to see his heavenly dwelling-place mirrored on earth.

There's more than a hint then that this city of Zion which the Bible talks about is also – in its fullest sense – a heavenly city with foundations, whose architect and builder is God, the very outline of which, as perceived with the eye of faith, was a constant source of wonder and joy to godly men and women. It's a city in heaven, yes, but one that in a sense casts its shadow on earth. The city of Zion on earth was – and will still be in the future – a shadow, a representation, of the real city in heaven where God dwells.

God's love for *"Zion above"* (Psalm 87:2) – Zion in heaven where his will is done – is such that it's led him to desire a representation of it on this earth in every age – including in the future when Christ will reign and be acknowledged as supreme. We've already learnt that Zion is the dwelling-place of God. God dwells above, of course – in the heavenly Zion – but in every age his desire has been to come and dwell on this earth among men and women whom he has brought together to do his will on earth as it is done in heaven. In every age, earthly Zion – whether a geographical city or otherwise – is modelled on the ultimate reality that's found in heaven itself, and this earthly representation can only be enjoyed collectively by those who take the Lord's commands seriously and give effect to them.

To see the truth of that last point, we only need to remember what happened to the nation of Israel, and to the city of Jerusalem or Zion in Old Testament times. When they failed to obey, and refused his warnings, and even his pleadings, God had no alternative but to use the Babylonians to discipline his people by taking them away captive for a while. But as we can see from the prophet Isaiah, when either the Assyrians or the Babylonians began to think too much of themselves because of their victory over Israel, God was well able to deal with them too – and cut them right down to size.

But coming back again to this thrilling and totally biblical idea of the earthly dwelling-place of God being modelled in every age on the ultimate reality that's found in heaven itself – whether that earthly representation is a physical city or some spiritual representation as it is today – it follows that there will be features of God's earthly dwelling-place which are common in every age in which men and women have served God. That's because what's on earth in each age is a copy of something that's unchanging in heaven. Perhaps, that's why the psalmist continued in Psalm 48:11-14 (NKJV) by saying this:

> *"Let Mount Zion rejoice, let the daughters of Judah be glad, because of Your judgments. Walk about Zion, and go all around her. Count her towers; Mark well her bulwarks; consider her palaces; that you may tell it to the generation following. For this is God, our God forever and ever; he will be our guide even to death."*

That makes me think of Paul's words to Timothy in the second verse of 2 Timothy 2: *"And the things that you have heard from me among many witnesses, commit these to faithful men who will be able to teach others also."* That relates to the idea in the psalm of describing 'spiritual Zion' to the following generation. On this our voyage of discovery, as I invite you to walk the pilgrim-ways to Zion with me, I hope to share with you several of these features of Zion's mirror image on earth – features which mark it out in every age and serve to draw our thoughts upward to the original and eternal dwelling place of God above – and even to God himself, of whom I trust that you, too, can say with the psalmist that he's your God forever and ever, and your guide even to death.

5

The Future of Worship

Jerusalem is never far away from the news these days. Divided between Jews and Arabs, it makes headlines for all the wrong reasons. The things that are spoken about modern-day Jerusalem are hardly glorious. In Bible-speak, present-day 'Zion' on earth is increasingly becoming a *"burdensome stone for the nations"* (Zechariah 12:3). What a contrast Psalm 87 paints with all of this, when it announces:

> *"His foundation is in the holy mountains. The LORD loves the gates of Zion more than all the other dwelling places of Jacob. Glorious things are spoken of you, City of God. Selah. I shall mention Rahab and Babylon among those who know Me; Behold, Philistia and Tyre with Cush: 'This one was born there.' But of Zion it will be said, 'This one and that one were born in her'; and the Most High Himself will establish her. The LORD will count when He registers the peoples, 'This one was born there'"* (Psalm 87:1-6).

The impressions made on us by that psalm – associated as it

is with the Zion or Jerusalem we know – are impressions of stability, prestige and the incomparable glory of the presence of God. Obviously, the time referred to is not now. The prophetic message of this psalm carries us forward to a time when the city of God's choice will be the centre of world-wide dominion. The absolute thrill that God has chosen Zion as his holy hill in preference to all others runs right through this psalm. God is there simply because he loves the place. And that's the source of its glory, stability and blessing.

Peace will come to Jerusalem, make no mistake. This psalm tells of a time when some of Israel's enemies will be reborn as citizens of Zion. Egypt and Babylon, two of Israel's greatest persecutors in history, will eventually be reconciled with her – together with Philistia, an ancient enemy, along with the trading centre of Tyre, and even distant Ethiopia. So, this psalm with its repeated reference to Israel's major Old Testament enemies, points to earthly Zion in the first instance, but it reaches its fullest meaning in terms of something still future on this earth – seen also from other Bible verses – a time when Israel's peace and prosperity will again spread to surrounding lands as in the golden age of Solomon, only more so. We can consider Isaiah's message in his second chapter:

> *"Now it will come about that in the last days the mountain of the house of the LORD will be established as the chief of the mountains, and will be raised above the hills; and all the nations will stream to it. And many peoples will come and say 'Come, let's go up to the mountain of the LORD, to the house of the God of Jacob; so that He may teach us about His ways, and that we may walk in His*

paths.' For the law will go out from Zion and the word of the LORD from Jerusalem. And He will judge between the nations, and will mediate for many peoples; and they will beat their swords into plowshares, and their spears into pruning knives. Nation will not lift up a sword against nation, and never again will they learn war" (Isaiah 2:2-4).

And yet, as we say these things over against the rumble of tanks and the screams of suicide bombers, you could be excused for asking: 'Is this prophetic vision of Israel's future peace and prosperity realistic? Maybe it's not meant to be taken literally?' Well, I'd just like to share with you what has always reassured me on that point – and it's this – another question: 'When Bible prophecies about Jesus the Messiah were fulfilled, were they fulfilled literally?' The answer is, of course, a resounding 'Yes!' – no matter how improbable they might have appeared beforehand.

But coming back again to our psalm, Psalm 87, with its mention of Zion, there's a definite hint of something else – something, that in ultimate terms, is also a heavenly and spiritual reality. Take, for instance, verses five and six again: *"But of Zion it will be said, 'This one and that one were born in her'; And the Most High Himself will establish her. The LORD will count when He registers the peoples, 'This one was born there.'"* I'd like you to compare Paul's words to the churches of Galatia in Galatians chapter 4:

"For it is written that Abraham had two sons, one by the slave woman and one by the free woman. But the son by the slave woman was born according to the flesh,

and the son by the free woman through the promise. This is speaking allegorically, for these women are two covenants: one coming from Mount Sinai giving birth to children who are to be slaves; she is Hagar. Now this Hagar is Mount Sinai in Arabia and corresponds to the present Jerusalem, for she is enslaved with her children. But the Jerusalem above is free; she is our mother" (Galatians 4:22-26).

"Jerusalem above ... is our mother." Remember that of Zion it will be said, *"This one and that one were born in her."* While recognizing that, in the future, nations previously hostile to Israel really will be reconciled to her, and Israel and Zion will be at the head of the nations in the centre of the earth – yet, now, more clearly glimpsed from this New Covenant perspective, we can see once again that heavenly or spiritual Zion refers to an ultimate reality, way beyond its earthly counterpart. The *"Jerusalem above"* mentioned by Paul is, of course, heavenly Zion - and he says it's the mother of believers in this age. How's that?

When we're born of the Spirit of God at the moment of putting our faith in Jesus Christ – after having turned away from our sins – then we're born, quite literally the Bible says, 'from above' - and it's certainly God's intention that we should be true 'sons of the New Covenant.' For Paul says that Abraham's wife Sarah symbolises the New Covenant in Jesus' blood which is identified with the Jerusalem above. Believers who are born from above have Jerusalem above for their mother and come within the scope of the New Covenant which replaced the Old Covenant God made with Israel. The Old Covenant directed Israelite paths to Zion on this earth; but now it's the highways to Zion above that should occupy our minds and command our obedience – and all this under the terms of the New Covenant made effective through Jesus' death. When that happens, it would be right for us to regard ourselves as 'sons of the New Covenant' - sons of the 'freewoman' if we're to go back to the apostle Paul's symbolism – and at the same time that makes us sons of Zion above.

Perhaps it's worth reminding ourselves again of the big idea that lies behind the Bible's use of 'Zion' which we're tracing mainly from the psalms. It's this, that beyond Jerusalem (that is beyond geographical Zion) there's a city where God dwells, a reality which exists in heaven: and the Bible calls it 'Jerusalem above' or heavenly 'Mount Zion.' And our spiritual and new Christian identity is given to us as being from there. As the apostle Paul could say to faithful disciples of Christ at Philippi: *"For our citizenship is in heaven, from which we also eagerly wait for a Savior, the Lord Jesus Christ"* (Philippians 3:20).

The New Testament urges us *"to set our minds on things above"* and it's in this sense we're encouraging each other to have our thoughts stirred towards the Zion above where the Lord Jesus Christ is already installed. If the highway from Sinai to Zion demanded the obedience of Israelites long ago, then how much more the highway to *"the Jerusalem which is above"* ought to claim the obedience of disciples of the Lord Jesus! Only careful obedience to our Saviour's commands will bring about the kind of Christian unity the Lord had in view in giving these commands.

Sadly, we vary in our obedience to the terms of the New Covenant and so professing Christianity is in a divided state on the earth today – just as the geographical city of Jerusalem is divided. How tragically different from the heavenly reality it's designed to model! And yet, on earth in every age, we should understand that God has a desire to dwell where there is an adherence to a unity of his own prescription – and his prescription is spelled out in those commands of his – and all designed to produce a unity which mirrors the perfection of the Zion that exists above.

6

The Centre of All True Worship

One of the great miseries of the modern world is the plight of refugees. It's a blight on human society and an indictment of modern civilization. It's one that points up our failure to live at peace and equality with one another. Some countries have millions of internally displaced people. Every single one will no doubt have their own tragic tale of being uprooted from their home and perhaps being torn away from their family too. Roughly about 600 years before Christ, the vast majority of Jews living in and around Jerusalem were deported by the Babylonians – who then, somewhat unreasonably, asked them to sing: *"For there our captors demanded of us songs, and our tormentors mirth, saying, "Sing us one of the songs of Zion!" How shall we sing the LORD's song in a foreign land?"* (Psalm 137:3-4).

Their captors demanded from them 'the songs of Zion': songs with which God had been honoured in connection with the temple-service back at Jerusalem. But it was as though the captives said: "How can we? It's the Lord's song; it's a sacred thing; it really belongs back home, not here. To have heard these songs sung in their intended setting must have been impressive. Zion where God dwelt was the focus of Israel's national worship of God, the centre of collective worship. With what great enthusiasm the songs of Zion must've been sung in and around Jerusalem! Psalm 9:11 gives the encouragement: "*Sing praises to the LORD, who dwells in Zion; Declare among the peoples His deeds.*" And Psalm 65:1 NKJV celebrates the fact that: "*Praise is awaiting You, O God, in Zion.*"

In a sense everything in Israel's national experience had been leading up to this collective temple service at Jerusalem or Zion: from that time in which they had first come to Mount Sinai as freshly liberated slaves. It was there, before that Mount, at the time of receiving the ten commandments, that they'd been absolutely overwhelmed by the awesomeness of God's presence. The New Testament's commentary on that experience described it in Hebrews 12:18-21 as a:

> "*... mountain that can be touched and to a blazing fire, and ... darkness and gloom and whirlwind, and to the blast of a trumpet and the sound of words, which sound was such that those who heard begged that no further word be spoken to them. For they could not bear the command, 'if even a beast touches the mountain, it will be stoned.' And so terrible was the sight, that Moses said, 'I am full of fear and trembling.'*"

If that was the effect of a real sense of the presence of God being known on this earth – one that was designed to bring them to worship God together in the Zion they knew in the land of Israel – what should be the effect on believers today who've been liberated from the slavery of sin with the intention that as a spiritual people for God we should be engaging in the collective worship of God in the Zion above?

Even Moses shook with holy fear that day. He'd drawn near before to that same place for his own personal encounter with God, but it was altogether different when it involved him drawing near with a people, a people who were to become worshippers together within the gates of Zion, ascending God's holy hill! It's the birthright of those who belong to the Lord today to have a counterpart to Israel's experience that's much more awesome still. The pages of our New Testament beg us not to despise this glorious birthright of our spiritual experience in the here and now. It lays it right alongside Israel's experience, when Hebrews 12:22-24 goes on to say:

> *"But you have come to Mount Zion and to the city of the living God, the heavenly Jerusalem, and to myriads of angels, to the general assembly and church of the firstborn who are enrolled in heaven, and to God, the Judge of all, and to the spirits of the righteous made perfect, and to Jesus, the mediator of a new covenant, and to the sprinkled blood, which speaks better than the blood of Abel."*

Tell me that's not awesome! When you think about it, we're talking here of a breathtaking privilege! For there's absolutely no doubt this is the Bible using the meaning of Zion that goes way beyond referring to any earthly hill or city – this is talking about the accessibility of heavenly Zion to us in worship when worship is according to the Bible pattern. This is Zion above portrayed as the real centre of worship, even now, for those who worship in spirit and in truth. That this is the true focal point of Christian worship must surely link it with our entrance as the worshipping people of God into 'the Holies' as described just slightly earlier in the same Bible letter of Hebrews: *"Therefore, brethren, since we have confidence to enter the holy place by the blood of Jesus."*

Privilege inevitably brings responsibility. Solemn responsibility, for it's an awesome privilege. But it's altogether a matter of our heart's affections. Psalm 87:2 says: *"The LORD loves the gates of Zion more than all the other dwelling places of Jacob."* Men and women after God's own heart have always developed an affection for the same things that the LORD himself loves. And the LORD loves the gates of Zion.

When we put it all together, here is the vision of those New Testament writers and disciples - that as they broke bread to remember their risen Lord on the first day of every week they had revealed to them that they were entering in some spiritual sense into the Holy Place in Zion above. The Jewish believers among them would perhaps come to see that their national background – as we glimpse it in the psalms and the songs of Zion – had only been preparing them for this better thing God had now provided them with – as he's also provided us with. For we ascend the holy hill of our God above – we come within the gates of heavenly Zion – to praise the God who dwells in Zion and declare his mighty deeds.

If it could be said of their Jewish ancestors in Psalm 84:7 that *"They go from strength to strength, every one of them appears before*

God in Zion" then what must it have meant to faithful Jewish Christians as they themselves gathered in first century New Testament Churches of God to remember their Lord Jesus and to enter the gates of heavenly Zion, so to appear before God in his presence above? Appearing before God! How could we even consider absenting ourselves from remembering the Lord in bread and wine whenever it's at all practicable for us to be there? Not just 'there' at the place where the church meets – but appearing before God in Zion! And if we're conscious, spiritually, of appearing before God in Zion - how much more should we attend to the question of Psalm 24, verses 3 and 4: *"Who may ascend into the hill of the LORD? And who may stand in His holy place? He who has clean hands and a pure heart."*

7

Worshipping in Zion Above

Let's think some more about Zion which, as we've seen, is the dwelling-place of God. I think you'd agree that one of the most important aspects of any dwelling-place is its foundation. And that has to be especially true of God's dwelling-place. And, in fact, Psalm 87:1-2 makes the point when it tells us: "*His foundation is in the holy mountains. The LORD loves the gates of Zion.*"

Perhaps many who sang these songs in ancient times would think of nothing beyond the actual foundation stones of earthly Zion in the Jerusalem temple – as when Jesus' disciples said to him one day: "*as He was going out of the temple ... "Teacher, behold what wonderful stones and what wonderful buildings!"* The magnificence of the stone-work in both Solomon's Temple and the rebuilt temple which Herod later improved, would have, and did, extend to the foundations – and God did dwell on earth in those temples – but the significance of that Psalm with its reference to the foundation of the Lord again surely goes way beyond anything in earthly Jerusalem, even beyond its future glory in the purposes of God.

In historical times of adversity, when the adversary threatened, God's purposes and plans remained rock-steady. In future times of adversity, when the adversary will threaten, God's purposes and plans will remain sure. For, at such times God looks to his kingly and priestly Son as in the words of Psalm 2 and verse 6: *"I have installed My King upon Zion, My holy hill mountain."* And he directs us to look there too. This is surely the cornerstone of all God's purposes. The foundation that nothing can overthrow or shake is this: God has installed his Son in Zion, in the seat of all rule and authority there. Nothing can challenge that. The foundation which the LORD has laid in Zion is his own Son, exalted above! He's set there as King; installed there as Priest – for ever in the ultimate seat of authority – which we've already seen is also the true centre of all worship.

The songs of Zion on disciple lips and hearts today magnify and glorify the One who's been exalted in Zion, for isn't that what Peter says when he talks about Jesus being foundational in God's Zion above? Jesus is described as the cornerstone. A cornerstone is, of course, an important stone, one often located in the foundation.

> *"Coming to Him as to a living stone, which has been rejected by men, but is choice and precious in the sight of God, you also, as living stones, are being built up as a spiritual house for a holy priesthood, to offer up spiritual sacrifices acceptable to God through Jesus Christ. For this is contained in the Scripture, 'Behold, I lay in Zion a choice stone, a precious corner stone, and he who believes in Him*

will not be disappointed.' This precious value, then, is for you who believe" (1 Peter 2:4-7).

The reference Peter makes to Zion, the dwelling-place of God, is in connection with its earthly representation in the spiritual house for God today that is made up of disciples of Jesus Christ who align themselves foursquare with the teaching of Christ. He's the Christ who, you remember, is pictured as the foundation or cornerstone (see also Ephesians 2:20-22). It's clear from the rest of Peter's letter that those he was writing to were born-again and baptized believers who were obeying the teaching Christ had delivered to his apostles. Fulfilling the Lord's requirements in these things was essential to satisfying the Father's longing for worshippers who would worship him in spirit and in truth. And worship that's in spirit and truth ties in with our understanding that the true centre of our worship is in heavenly Mount Zion where we offer up our spiritual sacrifices.

Peter says those who keep on coming to the Lord in the heavenly Zion are being built up as a spiritual house on the earth. Judging from how the Bible uses the same word elsewhere, it seems the act of 'coming' to the Lord in heavenly Zion is our 'drawing near in worship' - after all, it's the offering up of spiritual sacrifices which is being described. It would appear that this realization, the realisation that it's ours to worship in Zion above, is basic to the purpose of God's dwelling-place as represented on earth.

The whole process of disciple-making has in view this collective experience of worship in Zion above. The Lord's command in Matthew chapter 28:19-20 was: *"Go therefore and make disciples of all the nations, baptizing them in the name of the Father and the Son and the Holy Spirit, teaching them to observe all that I commanded you."* In this commissioning, the great imperative is to make disciples. 'Make disciples' is the main verb, the baptizing and the teaching are of necessity involved in the main business of disciple-making that prepares disciples to be worshippers after the Bible pattern. And the united service of such disciples today is in association with that Zion that's above.

God's dwelling-place – whether above, or as represented on earth – is the place where he not only resides, but where he rests and, yes, where he rules. For he's set his king upon his holy hill. All authority in heaven and on earth has been given to Jesus Christ. We could only expect that obedience should be required for us to have a part in God's house on this earth – and that specifically includes breaking bread to fulfil his command to *"do this in remembrance of me."* We've seen consistently in these studies that God's dwelling-place on earth in every age is to be viewed as the earthly representation of Zion: something on earth corresponding in pattern to what's in heaven above.

Notice again that it's a case of those after God's own heart valuing as precious the very same things that God finds precious. Peter says: *"to you who believe, He is precious."* He's talking of the Lord Jesus as the cornerstone, laid in Zion, and already precious to God. His preciousness to us is the theme of our praise within those gates of Zion, that're so beloved of the LORD. Remember, Psalm 87:2 says: *"The LORD loves the gates of Zion more than all the other dwelling places of Jacob."* It's altogether a matter of our heart's affections. Men and women after God's own heart have always developed an affection for the same things which the LORD himself loves. And the LORD loves the gates of Zion. I hope we are developing a greater affection for the gates of Zion.

Peter describes the Lord Jesus as the cornerstone laid in Zion above. And hopefully, we can see that this revelation which God has granted us through his Word, especially through Peter, is a progression of that same truth which the songs of Zion have declared from Old Testament times – as in the opening words of Psalm 87 - that "*His foundation is in the holy mountains.*" That was ever the focus, the theme, to which the united service of the New Testament Churches of God was directed. For, above and beyond even the glorious vision of a coming time on this earth when all God's purposes will be shown to be summed up in Christ, we've glimpsed again the glory of God's Son eternally established in Zion above. He's worthy of all our praise. Now, let's leave the last word to the psalmist in verse 89 of Psalm 119: "*Forever, O LORD, your word is settled in heaven.*"

8

The Pilgrim-ways to Zion

Isaac Watt's hymn "We're marching upward to Zion" is an uplifting one:

> *Come, ye that love the Lord,*
> *And let your joys be known;*
> *Join in a song with sweet accord,*
> *And thus surround the throne.*
> *We're marching to Zion,*
> *Beautiful, beautiful Zion;*
> *We're marching upward to Zion,*
> *The beautiful city of God.*

I hope the idea contained in that hymn will be a little more meaningful to us now. It's a hymn that seems to capture the joy of the pilgrims who long ago made their way to Jerusalem from all over the land of Israel; no doubt going up in pilgrim bands along the highways that led to Jerusalem. There's a group of psalms known as Psalms of Ascents, and one way to view them is as songs which expressed the longings of the pilgrims as they made their way to Zion for any of the appointed times of national worship at the Jerusalem temple. Psalm 122:1-4 captures this pilgrim character well:

> "I was glad when they said to me, 'Let us go to the house of the LORD.' Our feet are standing within your gates, O Jerusalem, Jerusalem, that is built as a city that is compact together; to which the tribes go up, even the tribes of the LORD – an ordinance for Israel – to give thanks to the name of the LORD."

There's another psalm that's not in this group, but which perhaps even more clearly pictures for us the state of longing in the soul of a godly Israelite whose all-consuming desire was to go up to meet with God at Jerusalem:

> "How lovely are Your dwelling places, O LORD of hosts! My soul longed and even yearned for the courts of the LORD; my heart and my flesh sing for joy to the living God. The bird also has found a house, and the swallow a nest for herself, where she may lay her young, even Your altars, O LORD of hosts, my King and my God. How blessed are those who dwell in Your house! They are ever praising You. How blessed is the man whose strength is in You, in whose heart are the highways to Zion! Passing through the Valley of Baca they make it a spring; the early rain also covers it with blessings. They go from strength to strength, every one of them appears before God in Zion. O LORD God of hosts, hear my prayer; give ear, O God of Jacob!

Behold our shield, O God, and look upon the face of Your anointed. For a day in Your courts is better than a thousand outside. I would rather stand at the threshold of the house of my God than dwell in the tents of wickedness. For the LORD God is a sun and shield; the LORD gives grace and glory; no good thing does He withhold from those who walk uprightly. O LORD of hosts, how blessed is the man who trusts in You!" (Psalm 84).

It's a 'song of Zion' with contrasting beatitudes. First, it declares the happiness of the person who's favoured with living in or around Jerusalem, perhaps with responsibilities in serving God: *"Blessed are those who dwell in Your house; they will still be praising You."* They wouldn't have to travel to be there in order to worship God. But not everyone could live there or be full-time engaged in Temple service, and the psalm goes on to recognize there were different blessings for the travellers as they made their pilgrimage to arrive in Zion: *"Blessed is the man whose strength is in You, whose heart is set on pilgrimage. As they pass through the Valley of Baca, they make it a spring; the rain also covers it with pools. They go from strength to strength; each one appears before God in Zion."*

The psalmist was gifted in seeing the blessing in contrasting situations: whether that of those permanently located at Jerusalem or that of those having to travel to get there. That's quite a lesson in spiritual contentment, isn't it? Sometimes it's easier to see the blessings of others. And we can end up counting our own hardships, not our own blessings. I was particularly struck by his description of the blessings of those who were travelling: *"Blessed is the man whose strength is in You, in whose heart are the highways* [to Zion]. *Passing through the valley of Weeping they make it a* [place of] *spring*[s]."

Isn't that a classic pilgrim statement of faith? The valley of Baca, where Baca means 'weeping,' is just so expressive of those valley experiences, those really low times in our lives. For we're pilgrims too, remember, for that's how the apostle Peter addressed his Christian readers. *"Sojourners and pilgrims,"* he called them. Now, pilgrims are pictured here making the valley of Weeping into a place of springs. Those springs of water would provide sources of refreshment and vitality. It was as though these pilgrims had to dig blessings out of hardships - the springs came out of the weeping. How was it that they were motivated to do that? I imagine it was the thought of Zion lying at the end of the journey that spurred them on, giving them strength – and that strength being from God – with which to overcome all the difficulties of the way. The strength came from the goal they had before them of "appearing before God in Zion." I wonder, what makes that same kind of perseverance possible for us as we journey upward and homeward today? Might it not be the vision of Zion for us also?!

The highways travelled in Psalm 84 were surely pilgrim-ways – that they led to Zion owes more to interpretation than trans- lation – but in the context that seems secure enough. and so we have the idea of 'the highways to Zion.' The teachings of the Scriptures are truly our highways to Zion. Through them it's revealed to us that the Israelite's experience in going up to meet God in Zion, as told out in these psalms, is a parable for our service as disciples of the Lord Jesus today. We've thought of the journey of rediscovery that brought Christians to see that there should be mirrored in Christian service today, something of the ultimate and eternal reality of his dwelling-place in Zion above. That journey was just like that of a pilgrim long ago passing through many hardships and arriving at length in Jerusalem, with feet standing at last in Zion!

But that journey – our spiritual equivalent of going from Egypt to Sinai – when once we make it our own, is really just the beginning of a weekly journey when Christians can ascend the biblical highway to Mount Zion above, the holy hill where God dwells and which is the true centre of all worship. Drawing near to God in worship is what's most expressive of our *"upward calling in Christ Jesus"* – when week by week, as we gather to remember the Lord Jesus in the way he's set out for us in our Bibles - we appear before God in Zion! So now, I hope, we can sing our pilgrim song with more meaning and fervour:

> *Come, ye that love the Lord,*
> *And let your joys be known;*
> *Join in a song with sweet accord,*
> *And thus surround the throne.*

> *We're marching to Zion,*
> *Beautiful, beautiful Zion!*
> *We're marching upward to Zion,*
> *The beautiful city of God.*

> *The hill of Zion yields*
> *A thousand sacred sweets,*
> *Before we reach the heavenly fields*
> *Or walk the golden streets.*

It's true that before we reach the heavenly fields, while still serving the Lord here on earth, we who love the Lord can enjoy the 'sacred sweets' of Zion. What experience is sweeter than to surround the throne above as worshipping pilgrims, with feet standing within Zion's gates, having come to Mount Zion, and having entered the holy place through Jesus' blood and merit?

9

Worshipping in Spirit

In some of our earlier studies, we made reference to John 4. Let's look a little more closely now at what the Lord Jesus said there about worship. Jesus said that true worshippers should worship the Father *"in spirit and truth"* – and then gave two reasons why: first, because the Father is seeking this kind of worship; and second, because God is spirit in nature (John 4:21-24).

Let's revisit the original setting of these words in John's Gospel chapter 4. One day, the Lord had to go to Samaria and there, by a well, he met a Samaritan woman. As well as offering her living water that day, Jesus, in the course of their conversation revealed to her a truth that has escaped many, and it's this: that the Father seeks worshippers who will worship in spirit and in truth (v.23). If we're familiar with the Bible, the phrase rolls off our tongue, but what did the Lord Jesus really mean?

The word 'spirit' here surely can't refer to the Holy Spirit. It would be quite wrong to imagine that others before this time weren't moved by the Holy Spirit in their worship; and equally wrong to imagine that our worship today can be any more the product of the Holy Spirit than the sweet words of David the psalmist. No, worshipping 'in spirit' here has to be different from worshipping 'by the Spirit' – which is also true, of course, as confirmed by Philippians 3:3 where the Apostle Paul says: "we ... worship by the Spirit of God and glory in Christ Jesus" (ESV).

Nor is this expression *"in spirit and truth"* simply conveying that a person must feel what he or she is saying in their own spirit; as a deeper experience than merely voicing words of praise. None of this denies, of course, that in worship our own human spirit does communicate with the Spirit of God. Mary, the mother of our Lord, gives us an example of that when she says in the so-called Magnificat section in the opening of Luke's Gospel: *"my spirit rejoices in God my Savior"* (Luke 1:47 ESV).

So far, we've learnt what the Lord **didn't** mean when he said we were to worship 'in spirit.' Before attempting to give our understanding of what the Lord **did** mean by that, we need to also consider his other characterization of worship as being *"in truth,"* for he spoke of worship that was both "in spirit **and** truth." There's a difference between truth and **the** truth, if by 'the truth' we mean the whole body of commandments of the new covenant, just as the law of Moses had embodied the commandments of the old covenant.

Quite generally, we may say that truth is very often simply the opposite of lies, but not in this case. What's true can also refer to something that's real and substantial over against whatever is merely shadowy or typical. As an example of this, remember

Jesus' words when he said, *"I am the true vine"* (John 15:1). A second example of this could be when the writer of Hebrews says at the start of chapter 10: *"For since the law has but a shadow of the good things to come instead of the true form of these realities, it can never, by the same sacrifices that are continually offered every year, make perfect those who draw near"* (Hebrews 10:1). Notice there how the 'shadow' has been replaced by 'the true form.'

If, then, the phrase Jesus used when he said *"in truth"* relates to that which is real and substantial over against that which is merely shadowy or typical, then we now need to revisit the parallel phrase in Jesus statement where he spoke about *"in spirit."* Perhaps we can conclude that this contrasts with worship that was previously 'in material things' in much the same way as 'in truth' – contrasts with 'in types and shadows' (which merely pointed the way to better things which arrived with Christ).

What, then, was the Lord saying to this Samaritan whom he wished to enlighten? His words "in spirit" refer to what has replaced the material ordinances, such as offerings and sacrifices, all of which existed in the time of the Old Testament, and which were only ever intended to be a shadow of the good things that were to follow. And, in particular, the Lord was indicating that physical venues at certain geographical locations such as Jerusalem or Gerizim would no longer be the all-important factor in this present Church age, as had previously been the case in the past, most famously at Jerusalem.

Consistent with that, those other words the Lord used to describe worship in the Christian era, namely 'in truth', were intended to tell us that worship is no longer in type and shadow, for such things had merely pointed the way to better things prepared for us in the time of the New Testament. God's requirements are no longer written upon tables of stone given to Moses or whatever else the Samaritans used on Mount Gerizim. God has now written his laws on our hearts, by the Spirit of God using his Word to direct us (Hebrews 8:10).

The English word 'worship' comes from an old word in the English language: the word 'worth-ship.' As the word suggests, it meant people acknowledging the worth or worthiness of who or what was being worshipped. Christian worship is a declaration of the worth of Christ, not with material objects or with the things of a physical house, like the Old Testament Tabernacle or Temple – but worship of God for his Son which comes from living stones built up as a spiritual house for *"a holy priesthood, to offer up spiritual sacrifices, acceptable to God through Jesus Christ"* (1 Peter 2:5), as the Apostle Peter says.

In other words, it was a double contrast that our Lord was making with the material shadows of old covenant worship when he spoke of worship that would be in spirit and in truth. He was broadcasting the start of a new era in which the key point would be a spiritual appreciation of the true nature of worship by disciples of Christ world-wide, yet all of whom would be associated in the one spiritual house. How marvellous to have an opportunity to be part of this!

I will comment more in our final chapter about the place where this worship actually takes place, but for the remainder of this chapter, I wonder if I could say a little about our daily preparation for worship when we come together in churches of God on Sunday mornings to proclaim Christ's death to God, to angels, to ourselves and to any visitors who have come to observe the proceedings. When the Lord was about to keep the final Passover at which he demonstrated the instruction given then to his disciples about how they were continually to remember him in bread and wine after he had gone back to heaven, the disciples asked him where he wanted them to prepare for this Passover celebration (Matthew 26:17,19).

Of course, they meant where they were to locate a suitable room and everything they would need, but it's good for us to have that question in mind as we approach the privilege, each Sunday, of entering God's presence while sitting around the Lord's table: Lord, where do you want me to prepare for this? Which Bible text should I use? We're looking to bring something of Christ – some grateful meditation of his person and work – to present in worship to God. Where in all the Scriptures (Luke 24:27) should we begin to prepare our thoughts? Yes, our canvas is as wide as the whole Bible!

Can we seriously doubt that Jesus explained to the two disciples who were going to Emmaus that he, as Messiah, was the Seed of the Woman; and the blessing of Abraham to all nations, even the sacrifice later to be seen in the mount of the Lord; that he was the High Priest after the order of Melchizedek; he was the one whose once-for-all sacrifice was foreshadowed by all of the sacrifices in Leviticus; he was the Man who wrestled with Jacob; he was the Lion of the Tribe of Judah; his was the voice from the burning bush; he was the Passover Lamb; and the Prophet greater than Moses; he was the captain of the Lord's army to Joshua; he was the ultimate Kinsman-Redeemer implied in Ruth; he was the son of David who was a King greater than David; he was the suffering Savior of Psalm 22, and the Good Shepherd of Psalm 23, despite being the Stone rejected by the builders?

He was the wisdom of Proverbs as well as the Saviour of the prophets and the suffering Servant of Isaiah who would give his back to the smiters (ch.50), whose face would be rendered humanly unrecognisable (ch.52), who would be numbered with, and wounded for, the transgressors (ch.53). He was Messiah the Prince of Daniel who would establish a kingdom that would never end, although he would also be 'cut off' (9:26), for Zechariah had said they'd look on him whom they pierced (12:10). And, of course, the Gospels tell us of the days of his flesh ...

Wherever we've been reading in our daily, systematic, devotional reading of the Bible should be able to supply us with worship thoughts that we can gather under the Holy Spirit's leading. It's good to have a pen and paper handy each day as we read, all the while praying that the Spirit of God will make real the things of Christ to us: that he will open our understanding, our hearts, and finally our mouths in Spirit-directed adoration of God's Son. Of course, this will demand that we first examine ourselves to ensure we are in the right spiritual condition (see Psalm 24:3-4 & 96:9; 1 Corinthians 11:28; Matthew 5:23-24 & 18:15) and with our hearts right with fellow-worshippers, and with no unconfessed sin between us and God (1 John 1:9).

Just as the Israelites long ago were commanded not to appear empty-handed before God (Exodus 23:15), we should realize that it is necessary that our high priest also has something to offer (Hebrews 8:3). There were times when an Israelite would come with an offering for God selected from the first and best of his crops and fruit (Deuteronomy 26:2). We can be sure this was presented as an orderly arrangement in a basket, an arrangement that quite some thought had gone into. As we each week bring and present "the fruit of our lips" to God, can we be any less careful about our presentation (Hebrews 13:15)? Long ago the Israelite was told (Psalm 96:6,8) to bring his offering, to come before God and worship. Shall we not do the same?

10

Worshipping in the Sanctuary

In the previous chapter, we were concentrating on Jesus' teaching about worship in which he said that true worshippers worship in spirit and truth. He was making a very distinct contrast with the ways of the Old Testament, with its physical structures, material robes and animal sacrifices. Our Lord was pointing to the spiritual nature of Christian worship. Christ's death brought about profound changes in the way we approach God in worship. It has moved us from the shadows of the Old Testament into the substance, the true reality, of the New Testament.

But even that realization of the spiritual nature of worship hardly prepares us for the revelation about New Testament Christian worship which we find disclosed in the Bible's greatest ever teaching letter, the letter to the Hebrews. To build up to what is surely one of the most stunning revelations about worship, the writer of the Hebrews' letter again reminds us of a bygone age, so as to make his point by way of a contrast. He says: "*Moses was faithful in all [God's] house as a servant ... but Christ [is] faithful as a Son over [God's] house – whose house we are, if we hold fast our confidence and the boast of our hope firm until the end"* (Hebrews 3:5-6).

In addressing himself to these Jewish representatives of the New Testament community which was then expressed everywhere in churches of God, the writer describes them as God's house, a term which, as the context clearly shows, answers to the Tabernacle in Moses' day. Now some of these people – and this was the whole point of his letter to them – were thinking about giving up. Persecuted, perhaps by other Jewish family members, they were finding their commitment to serving the Lord in the New Testament churches of God very challenging. They were beginning to feel that life would be a whole lot easier if they just slipped quietly back into the traditional ways of Judaism. The Bible writer, through the Holy Spirit, reminds them of what's at stake in this decision. He points out *"we are God's house"* but then adds: *"only if we continue to hold fast our confidence and our hope."* But, we might ask, what confidence and what hope was he referring to?

The best answers to these questions are found in the surrounding context. A few chapters later, we read: *"We have confidence to enter the holy place by the blood of Jesus"* (Hebrews 10:19); and also: *"This hope we have ... a hope ... which enters within the veil"* (Hebrews 6:19). As we said, we can only be sure of the answers if we read them out of the surrounding context, as we have done. And when we do, what we find is that there's a further confirming agreement, as the confidence and the hope which we find explained in Hebrews both relate to entering into a certain holy place. Understanding this feature of Christian worship is such a key thing that the writer's appeal is basically that "you must retain, as a matter of conviction, this belief that you enter into the heavenly holy place if you're to maintain your position within God's earthly house!"

Now, I added the word 'heavenly' there regarding the heavenly holy place – and you may say that I've not yet demonstrated from God's Word that this worship experience is in fact a present, heavenly one. Maybe you've read the words 'confidence' and 'hope' before in Hebrews, and understood them in terms of the basic hope of the Gospel that one day the Lord will take us out of this world and into heaven. Until such time, you've believed that the church worship service was a special time each week when our Lord came down to bless us with his presence on earth.

Let's see if simply using the Bible text as our guide, we can settle the matter of where exactly is this holy place into which God's people enter. Hebrews 9:24, which lies in between the two defining mentions of hope and confidence which we've just read, tells us: *"Christ did not enter a holy place made with hands, a mere copy of the true one, but into heaven itself."* Doesn't this make it clear that it's a holy place made without hands – in other words a holy place in heaven – into which Jesus entered in resurrection? Then we read: this is *"where Jesus has entered as a forerunner for us"* (Hebrews 6:20). Now, Jesus being the 'forerunner' implies we're now following on after him, entering into the place where he's already entered into - which is, of course, in heaven.

However, you may still be saying 'yes, but our entering in will be one day in the future after Christ's return, won't it?' Well, let's focus again on Hebrews 10:19 – *"we have confidence to enter the holy place by the blood of Jesus."* But the same word 'confidence' as we find here is used again in the same chapter, and in its other use we find that the warning *"not to throw away our confidence"* (v.35) is parallel with the other warning in this same section of chapter 10, which is the warning against *"forsaking our own assembling together"* (v.25). And that latter one was definitely a present experience for those Christians.

Let's recap: how were these first century Christians in the New Testament churches of God to retain their confidence? By making sure they kept on assembling together in the church worship service. It's a present assembling (v.25), a present confidence (v.35), and therefore a present entering into the heavenly holy place (v.19) when they assemble for worship. Entering the holy place – in corporate worship – is both a heavenly and a present experience! It's what answers to *"the way into the holy place"* (Hebrews 9:8) for a worshiping people today – and, of course, it's a spiritual experience, just as Jesus promised when talking to the woman at the well about worship that was *"in spirit and truth."* Now, to believe that takes faith.

Doubtless it's why we're told – in the same tenth chapter of Hebrews – to *"draw near ... in full assurance of faith"* (Hebrews 10:22). It takes faith to believe that as churches of God gather each Sunday morning around the Lord's table to break the bread in remembrance of him, that in presenting our worship we're actually, simultaneously, in some spiritual sense, entering into the holy place in heaven where Jesus our high priest serves before God for us. It's no coincidence that Hebrews chapter 11 is the Bible's greatest chapter on faith! It's sandwiched between two accounts of this experience which we're talking about!

The first account in chapter 10 we've dealt with, so let's turn for a moment to Hebrews chapter 12 as it expands on this same theme: "*You have come to Mount Zion and to the city of the living God, the heavenly Jerusalem, and to myriads of angels ... and to God, the Judge of all, and to the spirits of the righteous made perfect, and to Jesus ...*" (Hebrews 12:22-24). The overall theme of the Hebrews' letter centres on the corporate worship of God's New Testament people – remember it contrasts this with what happened in the Old Testament, using that by way of an illustration to explain what's really going on now – much of which is hidden to us because of its spiritual nature. Coming to Mount Zion, etc. is another description of what really does happen spiritually when Christians in biblical churches of God worship together God's way.

For sure, it takes faith to receive this revelation from God in his Word and, we say, that's no doubt why Hebrews chapter 11 majors on faith – simply because the surrounding revelation shared in chapters 10 and 12 requires a significant exercise of faith on our part. Finally then, what we're saying is that the Hebrews' letter teaches us that the corporate worship of the people of God on earth takes place spiritually in the real sanctuary that's in heaven. This shouldn't be totally unexpected because the Old Testament was meant to be illustrating for us how the then corresponding activity of national worship took place at God's material sanctuary on earth when God's people 'came together' at 'appointed times' (Exodus 23; Leviticus 23; Deuteronomy 16).

Answering to this, early Churches of God 'came together as a church' in order to 'break bread' (1 Corinthians 11-14) on the appointed occasion of the first day of every week (1 Corinthians 16:2) – so that's when they, too, enter the sanctuary now – which we've seen is a heavenly one. From the Old Testament story, we learnt the lesson that only at certain pre-set times did God ask his people to come together for corporate worship, and we also learnt that public corporate worship was located in the sanctuary. The sequel to all this in the New Testament concerns Churches of God coming together 'in church' at set times to break bread – at which occasions public corporate worship takes place in the heavenly holy place or sanctuary – of which the Tabernacle sanctuary on earth during Old Testament times was just a copy.

May such biblical considerations as this: of worshipping in submission, in service, in spirit and in the sanctuary – stimulate our faith and obedience as we respond to God in worship in the true Zion above according to the revelation of his Word!

About Hayes Press

Hayes Press (www.hayespress.org) is a registered charity in the United Kingdom, whose primary mission is to disseminate the Word of God, mainly through literature. It is one of the largest distributors of gospel tracts and leaflets in the United Kingdom, with over 100 titles and many thousands dispatched annually. In addition to paperbacks and eBooks, Hayes Press also publishes Golden Bells, a popular daily Bible reading calendar.

If you would like to contact Hayes Press, there are a number of ways you can do so:

By mail: c/o The Barn, Flaxlands, Royal Wootton Bassett, Wiltshire, UK SN4 8DY

By phone: +44 (0)7341 379815

By eMail: info@hayespress.org

via Facebook: www.facebook.com/hayespress.org

About the Author

Born and educated in Scotland, Brian worked as a government scientist until God called him into full-time Christian ministry on behalf of the Churches of God (www.churchesofgod.info). His voice has been heard on Search For Truth radio broadcasts for over 30 years (visit www.searchfortruth.podbean.com) during which time he has been an itinerant Bible teacher throughout the UK. His evangelical and missionary work outside the UK is primarily in Belgium, The Philippines and South East Central Africa. He is married to Rosemary, with a son and daughter.

Also by Brian Johnston

HEALTHY CHURCHES: GOD'S BIBLE BLUEPRINT FOR GROWTH

As Brian notes in the opening chapters, many churches in the Western world seem to be declining in numbers and spiritual vitality. He explores some of the root causes and also how this trend could be reversed. The good news, as Brian reminds us, is that God gives us the growth blueprint in His Word through a number of key Bible words, such as sowing, reaping, planting, watering, cultivating, building and edifying. Find out the importance of each step in the process and get inspired to go for growth with, in and through, God!

Can You Profess Christ and Still Be Lost?

The eternal security of our salvation is a hotly debated topic amongst Christians today. Brian examines what the Bible says about whether it's possible to 'fall away' and how God wants us to be sure that we are saved: 1) Law and Grace: Two Different Freedoms 2) Is It Possible To Be a Carnal Christian? 3) Is It a Case of 'No Holiness No Heaven'? 4) Are Good Works Required for Salvation? 5) Is It Possible to Fall Away? 6) It's Not About How To Be Saved 7) Is It Possible to Believe the Gospel in Vain? 8) Once Saved, Always Saved? 9) The Different Tenses of Our Salvation

Knowing God - Reflections on Psalm 23

Psalm 23 is also known as the Shepherd Psalm and it's one of the most-loved passages in the entire Bible. Brian Johnston links each verse to one of the God's names - a great way for us to get to know God better as: our provider, our peace, our healer, our righteousness, the One who is there, our victory banner, our sanctifier and our shepherd.

Abraham: Friend of God

What do you do when God wants everything you've got? That's exactly what happened to Abraham, the man to whom God also promised so much. Brian explores how it all came about and what was Abraham's response - although he's described as a friend of God and singled out for his great faith, his nomadic was far from plain sailing; there's a lot we can learn for our own journey of following God obediently as a disciple today.